Our Bodies

Sue Davis and Jeni Wilson

Contents

Parts of our bodies	4
Arms and legs	6
Our senses	8
How our bodies look	14
Inside our bodies	20
Our bodies work for us	22
My body	23
Questions	24
Glossary	24
Index	25

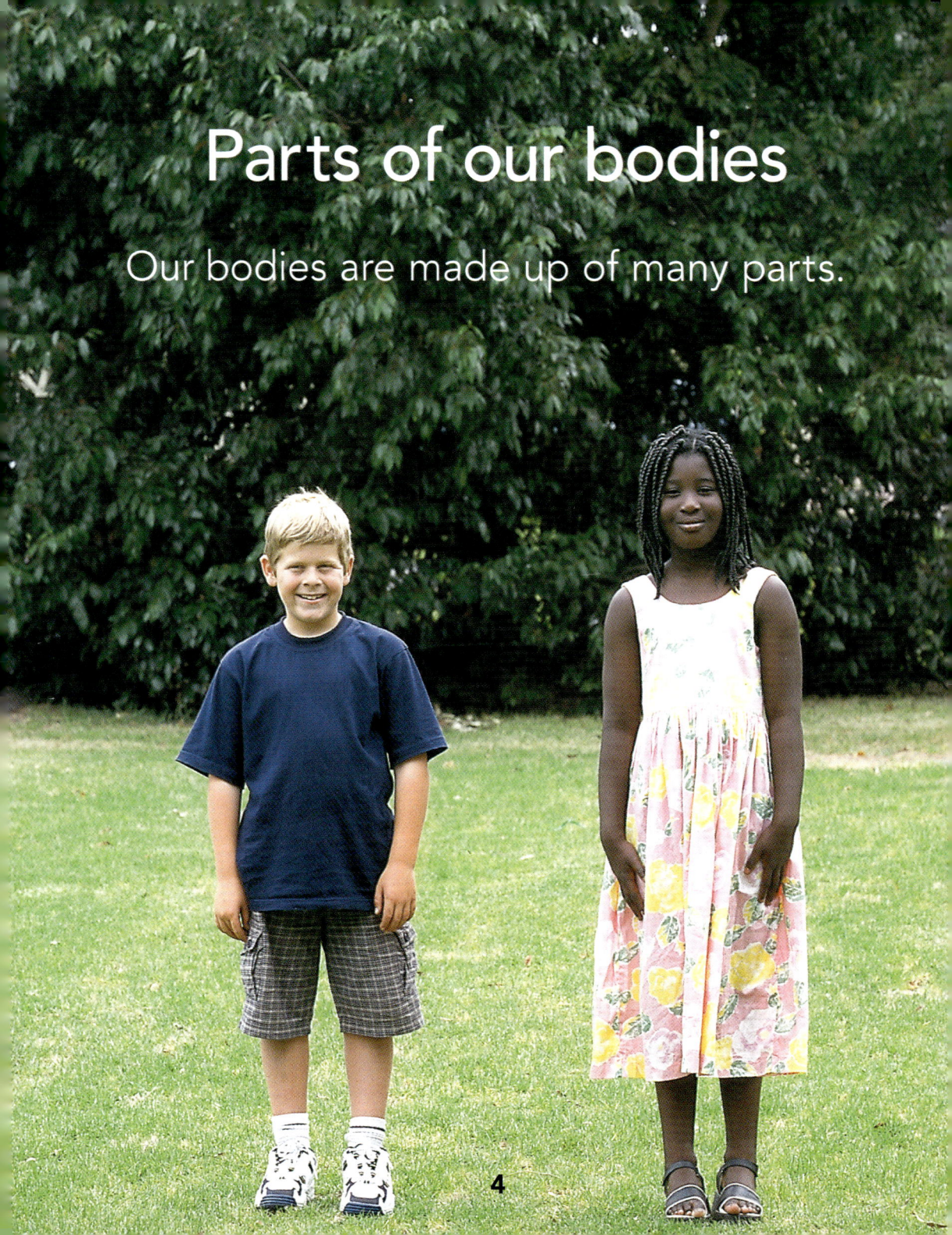

Parts of our bodies

Our bodies are made up of many parts.

Each part helps us to do all sorts of things.

Arms and legs

Our hands and arms and feet and legs help us to move.

We walk and run and kick with our feet and legs.

We can push and pull
with our hands and arms.

We can pick things up.

We can pat things.

We can
hold things.

We can clap
our hands together.

Our senses

We have five senses.
Our senses help us:

to **see**

to **hear**

to **feel**

to **smell**

and to **taste**.

Our senses help us to know what is going on around us.

Seeing

We see colours and shapes with our eyes.

Hearing

We hear noises and sounds with our ears.

Smelling

Our nose helps us to smell.

Tasting

Our tongue helps us to taste.
We like the taste of many things.

Feeling

We feel through our skin.

We can feel things that are:

hot or **cold**

wet or dry

hard or soft

How our bodies look

All of these children are seven years old.

Hair

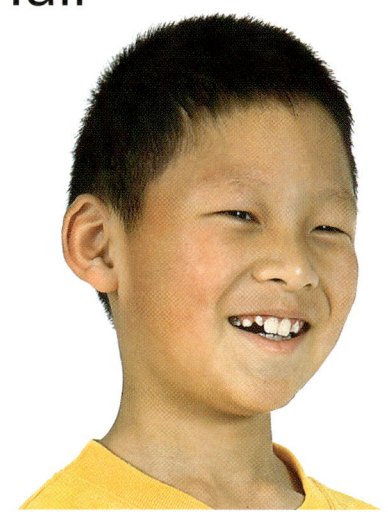 

Some people have hair like this.

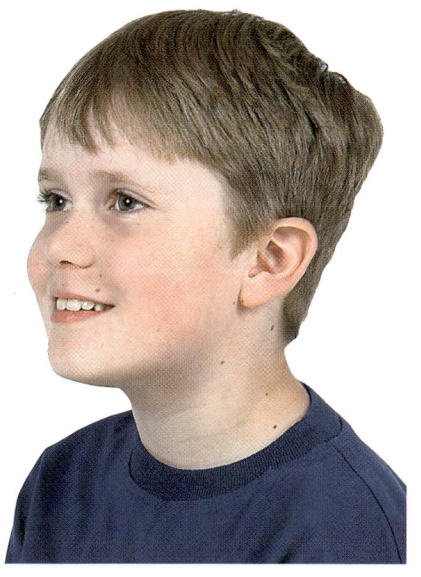

And some people have hair like this.

DID YOU KNOW?

Most people have blue eyes or brown eyes.

Eyes

This girl has blue eyes.

This girl has brown eyes.

Hair and eyes can be many colours.

Skin

We have skin all over our bodies.
Skin helps to keep
the inside
of our body safe.
As we grow,
our skin grows, too.

Our skin is soft.
It lets us bend and move.

If we fall,
we can hurt our skin.

When we grow old,
our skin can get
lots of lines.

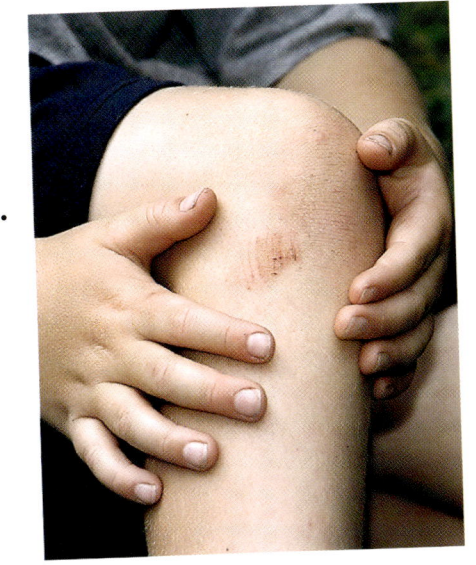

Inside our bodies

Inside our bodies
we have strong, hard bones.

Our bodies need bones
to help us stand up.
We have long bones
in our legs.
We have small bones
in our hands.

DID YOU KNOW?

There are more than 200 bones in your body.

Inside our bodies we have these parts, too:

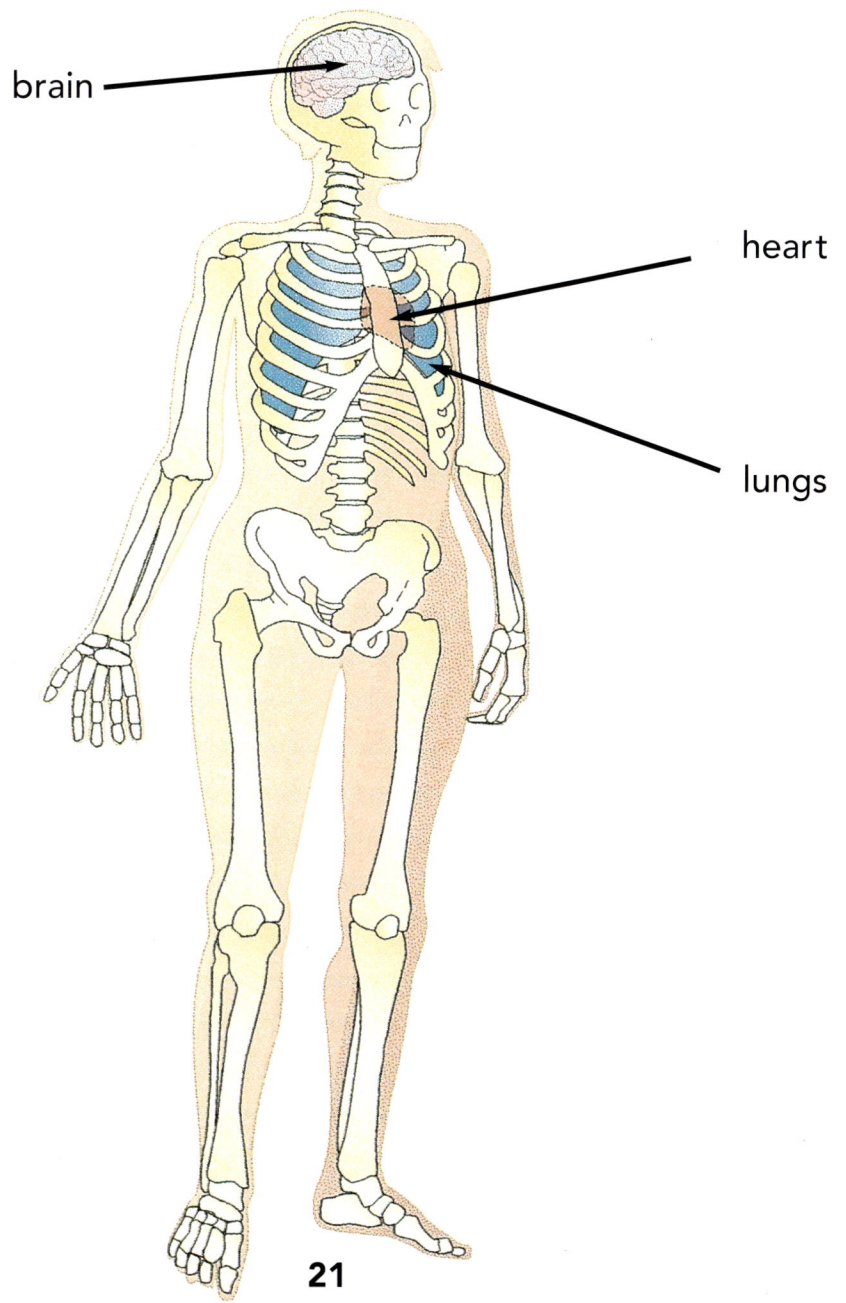

Our bodies work for us

Each part of our body has a job to do.

We need to take care of our bodies. Then our bodies can work well and feel well.

My body

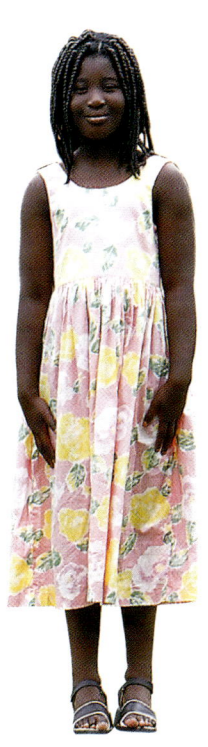

My arms have hands and fingers,
My legs have feet and toes.
My face has got two eyes, two ears,
A chin, a mouth, a nose.

And I can make my body move,
I run and jump and walk,
I sleep and wake, I laugh and cry,
I shout, I sing, I talk.

Jenny Giles

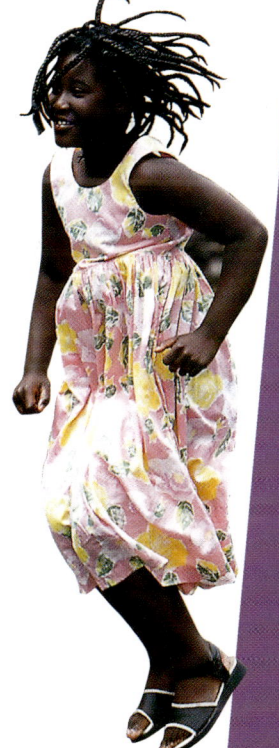

Questions

1. What are the colours of most people's eyes?

2. How many bones do you have in your body?

Glossary

part	*one bit of a whole thing*
hurt	*to be in pain*
bend	*to turn one way or the other*